ALMOST GONE

How Walgreens and the Pill Mills Nearly Took My Life

Robert B. Routt
Almost Gone Press

I0026776

Cover Design: Almost Gone Press
Interior Layout: Robert B. Routt
Author Website: www.robertroutt.com
Printed in the United States of America.
First Print Edition: 2025

Dedication

This book is dedicated first and foremost to **God**, whose grace carried me through a darkness I could never have escaped on my own.

To my parents, **Bob and Carol Routt**, whose love was the foundation of my life. Your strength, your faith, and your unshakable presence carried me when I could no longer carry myself.

To my daughter, my sister, and to the friends, nurses, doctors, family members, and loved ones who helped me survive, recover, and rebuild — this book is for you.

And to every person who prayed for me, visited me, or stood beside me during my recovery: thank you. You became the hands that helped pull me back into life.

This book exists because you refused to give up on me.

Acknowledgments

There are moments in life when everything falls apart, and the only reason you survive is because someone else refuses to let you go. I wouldn't be here today without the strength, love, and faith of the people who stood beside me during the darkest chapter of my life.

First, I thank God, whose grace carried me through places I could never have escaped on my own.

To my parents, **Bob and Carol Routt** — thank you for never leaving my side.

Mom, you talked to me every single day while I was in a coma. Your words, *"Bobby, show Mama those pretty eyes,"* reached me when nothing else could. I heard you, even when no one thought I could. Your love became the bridge that carried me back.

Dad, your presence never wavered. You steadied the room just by being there. When you told me, *"Come on, Son... Dad's right here,"* I fought harder. Your strength became my strength.

To my daughter, **Cynthia** — your voice was one of the first I recognized when I woke up. Hearing you say *"Daddy?"* grounded me in a way nothing else could. You gave me one of the strongest reasons to fight my way back into this world.

To my brother-in-law, **Steve** — you were there at the moment everything changed. You found me with my daughter and acted when seconds mattered. Your courage, presence, and quick action helped save my life, and I will never forget that.

To my sister **Carrie** — you carried our family so my parents could stay by my side day after day. Your sacrifice gave them the freedom to never leave me. Not all heroes wear uniforms; some carry families on their backs.

To my sister **Tammy** — you flew down from Kentucky to be close to me and to support our family. Your love and devotion gave us strength when we needed it most. Losing you in 2020 broke our hearts, but your spirit lives in every page of this book.

To my friend **Jill** — you came by almost every day and wrote down everything I said. Even when I drifted in and out, you never treated me like I was gone. Because of you, parts of this story were saved that I might never have remembered.

To my dogs, **Dutchess and Princess** — my loyal companions. Dutchess tried to wake me when my body had given out. Princess has been my shadow through recovery. Their love carried me in ways words can barely explain.

To the nurses, doctors, therapists, and staff at the VA Hospital — thank you for your patience, dedication, and humanity. You carried me through the impossible and helped teach me how to stand again, both physically and mentally.

To my girlfriend, **Erin** — your belief in me, especially when I didn't believe in myself, sustained me. Your love has been part of my healing.
And to my friend **Marc**, who brought me Outback when I couldn't stomach another bite of hospital food — it may seem small, but in that moment it was a lifeline. A reminder of normal life, comfort, and friendship when I needed it most.

To everyone who prayed for me, visited me, checked in, or refused to give up on me when I was at my weakest — this book exists because of you. I carry your love forward with deep gratitude.

Table of Contents

There are moments in life that split everything in two —
the life you lived before,
and the life you wake up to afterward.

For me, that moment wasn't dramatic.
There was no collapse in public, no flashing lights, no last words.
It happened quietly, in a bedroom, on an ordinary day.

My body had been pushed past its limits —
by pain, by pills, by trust in a system that failed me —
and it finally gave out.

I didn't feel fear.
I didn't feel anything.
Just darkness.

While I lay there, unmoving, my dog Dutchess tried to wake me —
scratching at my back, crying, refusing to give up on me.
She sensed something was wrong long before anyone else did.

Days passed with no answer from me.
When my mom couldn't reach me, she sent my daughter and my brother-in-law to check on me.
What they walked into wasn't a scene any family should ever have to see.

The paramedics arrived and checked my pulse.
Nothing in my wrists.
Nothing in my neck.
I was seconds away from being declared gone.

But a rookie paramedic — a kid barely old enough to shave — refused to give up.
He shocked me again. And again. And again.

On the **sixth** shock, something changed.
A faint flicker.
A heartbeat where there hadn't been one.

It was enough.

They rushed me out of the house, and I never saw it again.

From there, everything unraveled into a blur of lights, sirens, voices, machines, and silence.
A coma.

Surgeries.
The paralysis.
The fight to live again.

Everything that came after — the hospital rooms, the rehab, the fear, the hope, the slow climb back — started in that one quiet moment when my body gave out, and someone else refused to quit on me.

This is the story of what led to that moment...
and everything it took to come back from it.

CHAPTER ONE
Before Everything Went Wrong

Before the coma, before the surgeries, before the paralysis, before the near-death moments, I lived a life that—at the time—felt normal. Busy, stressful, tiring… but normal.

I was forty-seven years old.

Working fifty hours a week in the insurance business.

Carrying the pressure of meeting goals, helping clients, juggling deadlines, and trying to keep everyone happy. Most days felt like I was sprinting from the moment I woke up to the second I crashed into bed.

At home, things weren't any lighter. Problems I didn't want to face kept stacking up. Stress lived everywhere, my body, my house, my mind. I was moving so fast back then I couldn't see how close I was getting to the edge.

And the truth is, I was in pain. Real pain.

The kind that never lets up.

The kind that follows you from morning to night.

The kind you eventually stop mentioning because you're tired of hearing yourself say it.

Years of bowling—leagues, tournaments, endless nights repeating the same motion—had wrecked my back and my knee. But I kept pushing, because that's what I thought men were supposed to do.

Push through.

Ignore it.

Deal with it.

Pretend it doesn't hurt.

But pain doesn't care what you pretend.

Back then, I smoked. I drank. And yeah, I partied some. Not wild, not reckless—just enough to take the edge off, or so I told myself. I wasn't out running in the streets. I wasn't trying to escape my life. I was just a man hurting more than he knew how to admit.

Looking back now, the signs were all there.

The exhaustion.

The irritability.

The slow drift toward pills I thought were helping… until they nearly killed me.

At the time, I convinced myself everything was under control. I was still working. Still showing up. Still "fine."

But life rarely falls apart in one dramatic moment.

It crumbles slowly, quietly, piece by piece, until the weight becomes too much and everything finally gives out.

That's where this story really begins—those days and weeks before everything went wrong, when I had no idea how close I was to losing everything, including my life.

I didn't see the storm building.

I didn't understand how unprepared I was.

And I never imagined how far it would take me down…

or how hard I'd have to fight to come back.

CHAPTER TWO
The Slow Fall

Before the coma, before the surgeries, before the paralysis, before the near-death moments, I lived a life that—at the time—felt normal. Busy, stressful, tiring… but normal.

I was forty-seven years old.
Working fifty hours a week in the insurance business.
Carrying the pressure of meeting goals, helping clients, juggling deadlines, and trying to keep everyone happy. Most days felt like I was sprinting from the moment I woke up to the second I crashed into bed.

At home, things weren't any lighter. Problems I didn't want to face kept stacking up. Stress lived everywhere, my body, my house, my mind. I was moving so fast back then I couldn't see how close I was getting to the edge.

And the truth is, I was in pain. Real pain.
The kind that never lets up.
The kind that follows you from morning to night.
The kind you eventually stop mentioning because you're tired of hearing yourself say it.

Years of bowling—leagues, tournaments, endless nights repeating the same motion—had wrecked my back and my knee. But I kept pushing, because that's what I thought men were supposed to do.

Push through.
Ignore it.
Deal with it.
Pretend it doesn't hurt.

But pain doesn't care what you pretend.

Back then, I smoked. I drank. And yeah, I partied some. Not wild, not reckless—just enough to take the edge off, or so I told myself. I wasn't out running the streets. I wasn't trying to escape my life. I was just a man hurting more than he knew how to admit.

I didn't wake up one morning and find my life in pieces.
It didn't happen in one big dramatic crash.

The truth is, it happened slowly—so slowly I barely realized it was happening at all.

It started with the pain. At first it was something I could "push through." A bad day here, a rough morning there. I told myself it was age. Stress. Overwork. Old bowling injuries. Everyone hurts, right? Everyone deals with something.

But the pain got worse, and I did what most people do when they don't want to admit they're losing control—I tried to manage it quietly. I told myself I was handling it. That I didn't need help. That it wasn't that bad.

And that's when the pills entered the story.

Doctors prescribed them, and I trusted the system. I figured if a professional handed them to me, they would be safe. I didn't understand how quickly dependence could creep in... how easy it was to slip from "use" to "need."

I wasn't trying to get high.

I wasn't chasing anything.

I was just trying to feel normal.

One pill made the day manageable.

Two made it easier.

Three made it possible to get through the stress, the work, the responsibilities.

And on the outside, life still looked fine.

I was still working.

Still helping clients.

Still writing policies, returning calls, keeping my business together.

Still answering "I'm good" when people asked how I was doing, because the last thing I ever wanted was to look weak or needy.

But looking back now, the truth is obvious—the stress, the pain, the pressure, the pills... they were all hollowing me out from the inside.

I stopped sleeping.

I started losing track of days.

My moods swung in ways I couldn't explain.

My body was running on fumes, and I didn't realize how close I was to burning out completely.

And as things got worse, so did my judgment.

I trusted the wrong doctors.

I accepted medications I shouldn't have.

I believed pharmacies would catch dangerous combinations.

I assumed someone—anyone—would step in and say, "Stop. This isn't safe."

No one did.

And I didn't know enough, or feel strong enough, to stop myself.

People imagine addiction as chaos—screaming, spiraling, hitting rock bottom all at once. But that's not how it happens for most people. For most, it's quiet. Subtle. It sneaks in through the back door of your life while you're busy just trying to survive.

Painkillers were supposed to help me.

They were supposed to make my life easier.

Instead, they pushed me toward the darkest chapter of my life.

I didn't know it then, but the ground beneath me had already started to crack.

And every day, I was inching closer to the moment everything would collapse.

CHAPTER THREE
Pressure from Every Direction

By the time things really started slipping, I had become an expert at pretending everything was okay.

People underestimate how easy it is to hide a life that's falling apart. You stay busy. You keep moving. You smile when people expect you to. And you bury everything else deep enough that no one notices — not even you.

Work was a constant grind.

The insurance business can chew a person up even on their best day, and these weren't mine. I was tired, stressed, sore, and more dependent on pills than I wanted to admit. But the phone still rang. Clients still needed quotes. Policies still need writing. Life didn't care that I was running on half a tank.

Every morning, I told myself, *Just get through today.*

And every night I felt myself slipping a little further.

The pain was sharper.

The pills were stronger.

The gaps in my memory were wider.

I'd start a task and forget what I was doing halfway through. I would walk into a room and stand there, lost, trying to remember why I came in. Sometimes I'd catch myself staring at the wall, minutes gone, like someone had paused my brain without warning.

But stress doesn't back off just because your body is failing.

At home, things were tense — arguments, misunderstandings, a heaviness I didn't know how to escape. It felt like I was living inside a storm cloud, everything dark and heavy and closing in. I told myself it was just life… just adulthood… just pressure.

But deep down, something felt wrong.

Off.

Unstable.

There were moments — small moments — when I'd feel something wasn't right inside my body. A weird heartbeat. A feeling of floating. A sudden rush of heat. A moment of dizziness.

Looking back, they were warnings. Red flags everywhere.
But I brushed every one of them off.

"Just stress," I told myself.
"Just tired."
"Just need to push through."

The pills helped — until they didn't.
They masked the pain — until the pain returned louder.
They numbed the stress — until the stress multiplied.

And because they came from doctors, I didn't question it. Not enough. Not the way I should have.

I trusted the system.
I trusted the pharmacies.
I trusted that someone would catch a dangerous combination before it got to me.

No one did.

Some days I felt like I was watching my life from the outside, like I was floating just a few inches above myself, close enough to function but far enough away that nothing felt real.
I'd miss meals.
Lose entire hours.
Forget conversations.
Wake up feeling exhausted no matter how long I slept.

People around me noticed little changes — irritation, forgetfulness, zoning out — but they chalked it up to stress. And I didn't correct them, because the truth was harder to admit.

The truth was that something inside me was shifting.
Something dark.
Something dangerous.

And whether I knew it or not, I was sliding toward a point where there wouldn't be any easy way back.

The pressure was coming from every direction — my body, my mind, my home, my job — and I was scrambling to hold everything together with hands that were shaking more each day.

I didn't know it then, but I was standing on a trapdoor.
One that had already started to crack.

And sooner or later...

I was going to fall through.

CHAPTER FOUR
The Breaking Point

There's a moment in every downward spiral when things shift from "bad" to "dangerous."

You don't see it when you're in it — not clearly, not at first.

It feels like just another hard day. Just another problem. Just another flare-up of pain, stress, exhaustion, or frustration.

But looking back, I can point to the exact stretch of time when the floor beneath my feet started to give way.

The breaking point doesn't always look like a dramatic moment.

Sometimes it looks like silence.

Like numbness.

Like going through the motions because you're too tired to question anything anymore.

That's where I was.

The Medications Were Piling Up

The doctors kept prescribing. The pharmacies kept filling. And I kept trusting everyone except my own body. My pill bottles multiplied like rabbits — different colors, different labels, different purposes — but all with the same promise:

Relief.

Relief from pain.

Relief from stress.

Relief from the constant pressure inside my chest.

But the relief stopped working.

And instead of admitting something was wrong, I did what people drowning often do — I reached for whatever was closest, whatever kept me afloat for one more day.

Some days I took what I was supposed to take.

Some days I took a little extra because the pain was worse.

Some days I mixed things I shouldn't have mixed — not because I wanted to, but because no one ever warned me how dangerous the combination was.

My body knew before my mind did.
It started sending signals — warnings I brushed aside.
A sudden heaviness in my arms.
A wave of dizziness.
Moments where I'd lose track of what I was saying mid-sentence.
A heartbeat that felt like it skipped, stumbled, or paused altogether.
I'd sit down "for a minute" and wake up two hours later without remembering lying down.
But life didn't slow down just because I was unraveling.

Everything Was Coming at Me at Once
Work demands.
Family stress.
Financial pressure.
Physical pain.
The weight of years of pushing through things instead of dealing with them.
It all piled up until I could barely breathe.
Some days, even simple things felt impossible.
Getting out of bed.
Taking a shower.
Eating.
Returning calls.
Pretending to be "fine" when I wasn't anywhere close.
And still, I kept telling myself:
Tomorrow will be better.
Just get through today.
You're okay.
You're strong.
You can handle this.
But strength isn't infinite.
Even the strongest foundation cracks if too much weight sits on it for too long.

People Close to Me Saw It Before I Did

Little things gave me away:
A blank stare.
My hands shaking.
Me losing track of conversations.
The way I'd drift out mid-sentence.
The way I'd snap over small things, then feel ashamed afterward.
People asked if I was alright.
I told them yes.
People asked if I needed a break.
I told them no.
People asked if something was going on.
I shrugged it off.
Admitting the truth felt like admitting failure.
So, I hid it.
I hid everything.

But the body has limits.
And when it hits those limits, it doesn't negotiate.
It doesn't ask.
It doesn't warn you twice.
It just **stopped**.
The breaking point wasn't a single event — it was a series of tiny fractures.
Little cracks spreading under the surface.
Warnings I ignored.
Signals I pushed aside.
Moments where my body tried to save me and I didn't listen.
I didn't know it then, but I wasn't just tired.
I wasn't just stressed.
I wasn't just overworked.
I was dying — slowly, quietly, inch by inch.
And by the time I realized something was truly wrong...
I was already closer to the edge than I ever imagined.

CHAPTER FIVE
The Last 48 Hours

Looking back now, those last forty-eight hours feel like smoke — pieces, flashes, sensations. Not a clear memory. Not something I can recount moment by moment.

Because the truth is, I don't remember what happened when I passed out on Friday… and they didn't find me until Sunday.

Everything I know about those two days comes from fragments — what my body felt like, what people later told me, and the faint impressions my mind held onto before everything went dark. What I *can* say is this: whatever was going to put me in a coma was already in motion. I just didn't know it.

If the earlier chapters of my life were a slow decline, these two days were the drop straight off the cliff.

The First Day — The Body Starts to Fail

I remember waking up and knowing something was wrong. Not tired. Not stressed. Wrong.

There was a heaviness behind my eyes I can still feel today — like my brain had slipped into fog. My limbs felt disconnected, as if they were moving a half-second behind my commands. I told myself it was nothing. Lack of sleep. A bad night.

By mid-morning, dizziness hit in waves.
Standing up meant grabbing onto something just to stay steady. The pain in my back and knee was sharper than usual, and instead of slowing down, I did what I always did:

I reached for a pill.
Then another.
Then something to calm the dizziness.
Then something for the anxiety creeping in.

I wasn't keeping track.
I should have been.
But I trusted the bottles.
I trusted the system.
I trusted the idea that doctors and pharmacies wouldn't hand me

something that could kill me.

I was wrong.

By noon, I was drifting. Falling asleep sitting up. Waking up confused.

I'd stare at my phone, rereading the same text for minutes without understanding a single word.

Everything around me felt distant.

Muted.

Fading.

And even then, I told myself it was just stress.

The Second Day — When Everything Went Quiet

The next morning, what little clarity I had left was gone.

I felt underwater — heavy, slow, muffled.

My heart wasn't beating right. Too slow. Then too fast. Skipping. Pausing.

A warning sign that should've stopped everything.

But years of pushing through pain had taught me how to ignore danger.

So I tried to move through the day like everything was fine.

I remember trying to make coffee.

I dropped the mug.

It shattered on the floor, and I just stared at it... unable to decide whether to pick it up or sit down.

My legs felt unsteady.

My thoughts raced and then flatlined.

My breathing felt thick, uneven.

Then came the darkness behind my eyes — not sleep, not fatigue... something deeper.

A shutting down.

I told myself I just needed to rest.

Just a minute.

But a minute becomes an hour when your body is failing.

The Last Evening — The Edge

By evening, I wasn't myself anymore.

I was drifting in and out, losing chunks of time.
The pills weren't helping — they were killing me.
I remember trying to stand and my legs refusing.
I remember my phone buzzing somewhere nearby and being too weak to reach for it.

Somewhere deep inside, a small voice whispered that something was very, very wrong.
But everything else in me was too far gone to listen.

I laid down "just for a moment."

That moment never ended.

Those were my last flickers of awareness before the coma — a few scattered memories, a handful of sensations, and then nothing. My body shut down while I was alone, unconscious, unreachable.

I wasn't found until Sunday.

The next part of my story isn't mine to remember.
It belongs to my family, the doctors, the paramedics...
and a rookie who refused to give up on me.

CHAPTER SIX
The Moment I Disappeared

The last thing I remember from Chapter Five is the world tilting… the heaviness… the darkness closing in.

And then nothing.

I don't remember the moment everything went black.

I don't remember collapsing.

I don't remember the sound my body made when it hit the floor or the last thought that passed through my mind.

After those forty-eight hours of slipping in and out, of confusion and shutting down, there was no final warning. No chance to call for help. No dramatic moment of awareness.

My body simply… stopped.

Everything I know about what happened next comes from the people who found me — because I wasn't there anymore. My life kept moving, but I didn't.

The House Was Too Quiet

My mom had been trying to reach me for days.

Calls.

Texts.

Messages.

Nothing.

She said something in her gut felt wrong — the kind of signal only a mother gets, that silent alarm that doesn't care about logic.

When she still couldn't reach me, she sent my daughter and my brother-in-law to check on me. They expected to find me tired, maybe in pain, maybe overwhelmed, but alive.

What they walked into was something no family should ever see.

They Found Me Unresponsive

The house was quiet.

Too quiet.

They called my name as they moved from room to room.

When they found me, I was on the floor — unresponsive, pale, barely breathing, if I was breathing at all. My body looked like it had simply given out. My skin had gone gray. My chest barely rose.

My daughter called 911.

Her voice cracked.

My brother-in-law checked for a pulse.

Nothing in my wrist.

Nothing in my neck.

Those long, terrifying minutes are completely gone from my memory, but they stayed with the people who lived them.

The Paramedics Arrived Fast

Two paramedics rushed in — one seasoned, one a rookie.

They went to work immediately, but the truth was written across their faces. I was seconds away from being marked as gone.

They checked again for a pulse.

Still nothing.

The veteran paramedic turned to the rookie and said something like:

"He's too far gone."

But the rookie refused to accept that.

He shocked me once.

Nothing.

Twice.

Nothing.

Three times.

Still nothing.

By the fourth attempt, the veteran tried to stop him — told him it was enough.

But the rookie didn't stop.

He shocked me a fifth time.

Then a sixth.

And finally — something flickered.

Not a full heartbeat…

but enough to try again.

Enough to not give up.

Enough to save my life.

The World Moved Without Me

While all of this was happening — panic, shouting, electricity driving through my chest — I was nowhere.

I was deep in the dark.

Gone in a way that's hard to describe, because there's nothing to compare it to.

My family watched strangers fight for my life.

The rookie fought hardest.

My daughter prayed.

My brother-in-law stayed strong for her.

My mom waited for a phone call that could have shattered her.

I was lifted onto a stretcher.

Loaded into the ambulance.

Rushed through the streets with lights and sirens.

Everyone else was fighting for me.

I wasn't there to feel any of it.

The End of Who I Had Been... the Start of Who I Would Become

When my body collapsed, my old life collapsed with it — the pills, the pain, the denial, the years of pushing through instead of reaching out. All of it ended in that silent house.

Everything that happened afterward — the coma, the surgeries, the paralysis, the recovery — began in that moment where my life broke wide open.

I didn't know it then, but that was the turning point.

The final chapter of the old me.

The first chapter of the man who would have to rebuild everything from the ground up.

What came next wasn't survival — it was a fight.

And it was only just beginning.

CHAPTER SEVEN
Inside the Coma

People think a coma is just sleep — a deep, silent, peaceful sleep.

They imagine darkness and stillness and nothing else.

They're wrong.

A coma is its own universe.

A place where time doesn't make sense.

A place where your mind floats without gravity.

A place where you are both nowhere and everywhere at the same time.

I wasn't dead.

But I wasn't alive in any way that felt real either.

I existed in a space between.

The Darkness

At first, there was only darkness.

Not the kind you get when you turn off a light — this was heavier, thicker, like a blanket pressed over my entire existence.

I didn't know where I was.

I didn't know what had happened.

I didn't know if I was awake or gone or dreaming.

I just… was.

No pain.

No fear.

No understanding.

Just a deep, endless black.

But even in that emptiness, something reached me.

The Voices

The first thing that broke through was my mom's voice.

"Bobby… show Mama those pretty eyes."

I didn't see her.

I didn't feel her.

But her voice cut through the darkness like a warm light.

It wrapped around me, pulled me toward something familiar,

something safe.
Then I heard my dad:
"Come on, Son... Dad's right here."
His voice was steady. Strong.
Even in the coma, it grounded me.
I didn't have words.
I couldn't respond.
I couldn't open my eyes.
But somewhere deep inside the blackout, I recognized them.
And then... I heard my daughter.
"Daddy?"
Her voice was soft, scared, breaking — and it cut through me in a way nothing else could.
It was the first voice I truly knew.
The first one that didn't just sound familiar — it brought me back to myself.
I wasn't dead.
Not yet.
Not as long as I could still hear her.

Flashes of Light, Shadows, and Something Like Dreams
I drifted in and out of moments that didn't make sense:
A bright light overhead.
Cold air on my skin.
The feeling of being lifted.
Machines beeping.
Hands on my chest.
A siren.
A door closing.
Someone shouting numbers.
Something sharp pressing into my arm.
A mask over my face.
Then darkness again.
Time dissolved.
Minutes felt like hours.
Hours felt like seconds.

Days passed without me noticing.
But sometimes… there were dreams.
Strange dreams.
Fragments of places I'd been or people I loved.
Dutchess scratching at my back like she had that day.
The bowling alley lights flickering in odd patterns.
My dad's hand on my shoulder.
Dreams that felt real enough to touch.
Dreams that weren't dreams at all — more like memories floating loose in the dark.

The Outside World

While I drifted somewhere between life and death, the people who loved me were living through the nightmare I couldn't see.
My mom talked to me every day, hoping her voice would reach the part of me that was still hanging on.
My dad stood beside my bed, gripping the rail, whispering strength into me.
My daughter cried, prayed, begged me to come back.
Carrie held the family business together so my parents never had to leave the hospital.
Tammy flew down from Kentucky and stayed close, not knowing if she would ever hear my voice again.
Jill came by, checking on me, telling stories, talking to me like I could answer.
I didn't hear every word.
But I felt the presence.
The warmth.
The love.
The pressure of hands on my arm.
The sound of tears being wiped away.
The whisper of hope and fear tangled together.
Something inside me held on for them.

More Than a Body

When you're trapped inside a coma, your body isn't yours.

It's a thing being moved, prodded, monitored, kept alive by machines and people you can't see.

But your mind — or whatever part of your soul stays awake — drifts freely.

I floated between worlds.

One where I felt weightless.

One where I heard muffled voices.

One where I felt echoes of pain that didn't quite reach me.

One where time didn't matter.

I wasn't ready to die.

But I wasn't strong enough to live either.

I just existed in the in-between.

The Moment Before Waking

There was no dramatic surge. No movie-style awakening.

It started with a flicker — a spark of awareness, a sense that something was shifting.

Light pressed against the darkness.

Voices grew clearer.

The world started to pull at me instead of drift away.

I don't know what triggered the moment.

But I do know who kept me alive long enough to reach it:

My family.

My friends.

The rookie paramedic who refused to give up.

And God — because there's no earthly explanation for me surviving what I did.

When I finally opened my eyes, the world was bright, blurry, overwhelming.

But the first thing I heard clearly was the voice that had been echoing in my darkness:

"Daddy?"

And for the first time in weeks,

I answered.

CHAPTER EIGHT
Waking Up

Waking up wasn't like opening my eyes after a long sleep.

It wasn't peaceful.

It wasn't gentle.

It wasn't even clear.

It was like being dragged upward through thick water — heavy, slow, disorienting — until suddenly, the surface shattered and everything hit me at once.

Light.

Sound.

Pain.

Voices.

Machines.

Fear.

The world didn't come back into focus — it came back like a punch.

The First Moments

The lights were too bright.

My vision blurred, then doubled, then drifted out of focus.

For a moment, I didn't know where I was.

I didn't know who I was.

My body didn't feel like my own.

Everything was heavy.

My chest hurt.

My throat burned like someone had shoved sandpaper down it.

My left side felt wrong — numb and distant, like it belonged to someone else.

I tried to move and nothing happened.

Not my fingers.

Not my arm.

Not my leg.

Fear rose in my throat faster than I could understand it.

A sound escaped me — not a word, not a cry, just a broken

noise.

Then a voice cut through everything.

"Dad…? Daddy?"

My daughter's voice.

It anchored me in a way nothing else could.

It cracked through the haze and pulled something inside me toward the surface.

I blinked.

And for the first time, the blur in front of me sharpened just enough to make out shapes — her silhouette, my parents behind her, the outlines of nurses moving around me.

My daughter leaned in close.

Tears in her eyes.

Hope in her voice.

Fear under all of it.

"Daddy… can you hear me?"

I tried to answer.

My lips moved, but nothing came out.

The fear in her eyes shifted into relief — because even that tiny movement meant something.

The World Was Loud

Machines beeped in chaotic rhythms.

Nurses called out instructions.

Something hissed beside my bed.

Someone adjusted a tube in my nose.

Someone else checked a monitor.

Every sound felt too loud, too close, too intense.

My heart pounded.

My breathing was uneven.

My head felt like it was filled with lead.

And then came the pain.

Sharp.

Deep.

Everywhere.

Pain in my chest from being shocked.
Pain in my throat from tubes.
Pain in my muscles from not moving for weeks.
Pain in my left side that felt like absence more than sensation.

I wanted to cry out, but the only thing that came was another broken noise.

The Room Around Me

I could see my mom standing by the bed, tears streaming down her face.
She took my hand even though it couldn't grip hers back.
"Bobby… show Mama those pretty eyes."
The same words she whispered into the darkness of my coma.

My dad stood strong — jaw tight, eyes red, refusing to break down in front of me.
"Come on, Son… Dad's right here."

You don't understand how powerful those words are until you hear them when you're halfway between life and death.

A nurse leaned in, checking my vitals, speaking softly.
"Robert, you're in the hospital. You were very sick, but you're safe now. You're doing good. Just breathe, okay? Just breathe."

But nothing felt safe.
Nothing felt real.
The world looked tilted, too bright, too loud, too much.

Trying to Understand

Pieces of memory flickered in my mind — shadows, voices from the coma, the sound of my dog, the feeling of sinking.
None of it made sense.

I tried to speak, to ask what happened, but my voice wouldn't come.
My throat burned too badly.
My body wasn't responding.

The nurse saw the fear in my eyes and gently explained what had happened — slowly, carefully, like talking to someone learning how to exist again.

"Your heart stopped. You were unresponsive. Paramedics revived you. You've been in a coma. You're okay now, but you need to rest. You're safe."

I heard the words.

They didn't feel real.

They felt like a story someone else lived.

I didn't know yet how bad things were — the paralysis, the long road ahead, the months of recovery.

All I knew was that I wasn't dead.

And that felt like both a blessing and a shock.

Relief, Fear, and Something Else

There was relief — a deep, overwhelming wave of it — but it mixed with fear so intense it was hard to breathe.

I didn't know what was wrong with my body.

I didn't know why I couldn't move my left side.

I didn't know how close I'd come to dying.

But I knew one thing for sure:

My family had been there the entire time.

Their faces, their voices, their hands holding mine — they were the bridge between the world I'd been trapped in and the world I was returning to.

In that moment, I didn't know if I'd walk again.

I didn't know if my memory would come back.

I didn't know what the next chapter of my life would look like.

But I was awake.

I was alive.

And I wasn't alone.

And sometimes, that's enough.

CHAPTER NINE
The Medical Reality

When you wake up from a coma, you don't get the full story right away.

The world comes back in pieces — like a puzzle dumped across a table, scattered in every direction.

Doctors don't walk in with a neat explanation tied in a bow.

They give it to you slowly, carefully, watching your face to make sure you don't break.

I didn't understand any of it at first.

My mind wasn't steady.

My body felt foreign.

My memory was fogged, blurry, unreliable.

All I knew was that something was wrong with me.

Badly wrong.

The Doctors' First Conversation With Me

A doctor stood at the foot of my bed — calm, professional, the type of person who's had this conversation too many times.

He spoke gently, like someone delivering news to a man who might not be strong enough to hear it.

"Robert… you went into cardiac arrest at home.

When the paramedics arrived, you didn't have a pulse. You were resuscitated.

You were in a coma for several weeks."

His voice was steady, almost rehearsed, but the words hit me like punches.

Cardiac arrest.

No pulse.

Coma.

I stared at him, trying to make the words fit together.

They didn't.

Not at first.

He continued:

"You were found unresponsive. You were revived by a

paramedic — a new one, actually — who refused to stop trying. You're very fortunate he insisted."

I blinked, trying to comprehend the weight of what he said.

A rookie saved my life.

Six shocks to bring me back.

Seconds from being declared gone.

The doctor waited, giving me time to process.

But I couldn't.

How do you process the fact that you were dead and didn't know it?

The Pills — The Hardest Part to Hear

The doctor approached slowly, concern etched across his face.

"Your toxicology panel showed multiple medications in your system. Some of them interacted in dangerous ways. Your body couldn't keep up."

I felt a different kind of pain — not physical, but shame mixed with fear.

I hadn't been trying to hurt myself.

I wasn't chasing a high.

I was trying to numb pain that wouldn't stop.

But I trusted the wrong doctors.

I trusted the wrong pharmacies.

I trusted pills that should never have been combined.

The doctor explained what the mixture had done:

Suppressed my breathing.

Slowed my heart.

Decreased oxygen to the brain.

Caused the collapse.

Every word added a new layer of guilt and confusion.

It wasn't intentional…

but it was dangerous.

And I was paying the price.

Then Came the Hardest Truth

The doctor stepped closer, voice softer:

"Robert… you have partial paralysis on your left side."

My heart dropped.

"What do you mean?" I tried to ask, but it came out weak, barely audible.

He continued:

"You suffered a neurological event during the cardiac arrest. A stroke.

The lack of oxygen caused damage. That's why you can't move your left arm and leg."

The words washed over me like cold water.

Left side paralysis.

Stroke.

Neurological damage.

I tried to move my left hand.

Nothing.

I tried to lift my leg.

Nothing.

The fear that hit me was deeper than anything I had ever felt.

A thousand thoughts rushed through me:

Will I walk again?

Will I be the same?

Is this permanent?

How did I let this happen?

What will my life look like now?

The doctor saw the panic and softened his tone.

"It's too early to know what will come back.

You're stable now, and that's what matters.

Rehab will be the next step."

Rehab.

I didn't even know what that meant yet.

My Family Got More Truth Than I Did

Later, I learned the doctors had given my family their own version of the truth:

"He may not wake up."

"He may have brain damage."

"He may never walk again."

"He may never regain movement on the left side."

"He may not survive the night."

My parents and daughter lived through hell while I drifted in a darkness I can barely remember.

They held onto hope when I had none.

They prayed, cried, begged — all while machines kept me breathing and strangers kept me alive.

Hearing what they went through was almost harder than hearing what happened to me.

Facing Reality

Lying in that hospital bed, a new reality settled in:

I wasn't the same man who collapsed in that house.

My body was different.

My mind was different.

My life was different.

The world felt unfamiliar — both too loud and too quiet at the same time.

But one thing was clear:

If I was going to survive — really survive — I had a long road ahead.

A road filled with pain, frustration, therapy, setbacks, tiny victories, and moments where I would wonder if I'd ever get back to anything that felt like myself.

The coma was the storm.

Waking up was the wreckage.

Now it was time to face the damage.

And begin to rebuild.

CHAPTER TEN
The Left Side That Wouldn't Move

The mind wakes up long before the body does.

In those first days after the coma, I felt like a man trapped inside himself — aware enough to see the world, but not strong enough to reach out and touch it.

Nothing prepared me for the moment I realized my left side wasn't working.

Not the doctors' warnings.

Not the numb heaviness.

Not the strange disconnect I felt when I opened my eyes.

It wasn't real until I tried to move.

The First Attempt

A nurse asked me to lift my left arm.

She said it gently, like she already knew what was coming.

I looked at my arm.

It looked normal — bruised, swollen, pale — but still mine.

I told my brain to lift it.

Nothing happened.

I tried again.

Harder.

I focused until my head throbbed.

Still nothing.

My arm just lay there, heavy as concrete, refusing to move even an inch.

A tight panic rose in my chest.

I turned to the nurse, hoping she'd tell me to try again, that it was just weakness, that it was temporary.

Instead, she gave me a sympathetic nod.

"It's okay, Robert. We'll take it one step at a time."

But it wasn't okay.

Not even close.

The Leg Was Worse

When they asked me to move my left leg, I already knew what would happen.

Nothing.

Not a twitch.

Not a shift.

Not even the slightest signal that my brain and my body were still connected.

It felt like half of me had been erased.

I wasn't just weak — I was disconnected.

Like someone had unplugged the entire left side of my body.

The silence in that limb was terrifying.

The Emotional Collapse

The doctor tried to explain again:

"Your stroke happened during the cardiac arrest.

The lack of oxygen caused injury to the motor pathways on the right side of your brain.

That's why the left side is affected."

He said it in the calm, professional tone doctors use when the truth is too sharp to deliver plainly.

I heard every word, but my mind got stuck on one thing:

I might never move my left side again.

It hit me like a weight.

My eyes burned.

My throat tightened.

I felt tears leak out before I could stop them.

I wasn't crying from pain — I was crying from fear.

Fear of never walking again.

Fear of needing help for basic things.

Fear of never being the same man I used to be.

Fear that I had done this to myself by trusting the wrong pills, the wrong doctors, the wrong instincts.

A nurse squeezed my hand — my *right* hand — the only one that could respond.

"Robert... you're alive. That's the starting point. Everything else comes one step at a time."

I nodded, but the truth was already sinking in:

This wasn't going to be a quick recovery.

This wasn't going to be a week in bed and back to normal.

This was going to take everything I had.

Trying Again

Later that day, alone with my own thoughts, I tried again.

I stared at my left fingers, willing them to move.

Just twitch, I begged silently.

Just one twitch. Just one sign that you're still there.

Nothing.

My heart sank.

I tried to lift my forearm.

Nothing.

I tried to shift my leg.

Still nothing.

The helplessness was overwhelming — a kind of vulnerability I had never felt before.

I had always been the one who handled things.

The one who worked through pain.

The one who pushed no matter what.

But this was a battle I couldn't "push through."

This was something different — something bigger than willpower.

Something broken deep inside my body.

The Hardest Question

When the doctor came back, I finally asked the question that had been eating at me since the moment I woke up.

"Will I walk again?"

He paused — too long.

"We don't know yet," he said carefully.

"It depends on your brain's ability to reroute pathways. Rehab can help. Progress varies from person to person."

Not yes.

Not no.

Just **uncertainty** — the one thing I feared most.

But then he added:

"You woke up. That already means you're a fighter. Don't underestimate that."

The First Sign of Hope

Hours later, when the room was quiet and I was alone, something small happened.

I felt the faintest flicker — not movement, but a sensation — like someone lightly brushing the outside of my left foot.

It wasn't much.

It wasn't dramatic.

It wasn't even movement.

But it was *something.*

A whisper of life where there had been silence.

And in that moment, that tiny flicker felt like hope.

CHAPTER ELEVEN
The First Days of Rehab

Rehab didn't feel like recovery.

Not at first.

It felt like punishment — like a reminder of everything I had lost and everything I didn't know how to get back. Every movement hurt. Every exercise reminded me that half my body wasn't working. Every attempt felt like an uphill climb on legs that didn't belong to me.

But rehab wasn't optional.

It was the line between my old life… and any chance at a new one.

And even though I didn't know it then, those first brutal days were the foundation for everything that came afterward.

Meeting the Rehab Team

The therapists came into my room the morning after the doctor told me about the paralysis.

There were three of them:

A physical therapist with a no-nonsense look.

An occupational therapist with calm, patient eyes.

And an assistant who had the kind of encouraging smile that made you feel stupid for wanting to give up.

They introduced themselves, explained their roles, and then asked a question I didn't want to hear:

"You ready to get started?"

I wasn't ready.

Not mentally.

Not physically.

Not emotionally.

But rehab doesn't care if you're ready.

It only cares if you're willing.

So I nodded.

Sitting Up for the First Time

They helped me sit up in bed — something I had done

thousands of times before without thinking.

But this time, it felt like a battle.

My right side did all the work.

My left side hung there — dead weight.

The room tilted.

My head pounded.

My breathing tightened.

My legs dangled over the edge of the bed, and I realized how much of my balance had vanished.

I felt like a child learning how to exist in his own body.

A therapist put a hand on my back.

"You're doing good."

But I didn't feel good.

I felt weak, embarrassed, and afraid.

The First Stand

When they told me to try standing, my heart dropped.

"How?" I asked.

"Your right leg is strong," the therapist said.

"We'll support your left. Just trust us."

Trust.

That was the hardest part.

With two therapists holding me at my sides and one guiding my left leg, I pushed through my right foot and tried to stand.

My body trembled.

My vision blurred.

My left leg gave nothing.

But somehow — with their arms holding me up — I got vertical.

I stood.

It wasn't pretty.

It wasn't independent.

But I stood.

And that tiny moment felt like a crack of light in a very dark room.

Frustration Hits Hard

That first session drained everything out of me.

By the time they helped me back into bed, I could barely keep my eyes open.

But the real blow came later, when the adrenaline wore off.

I stared at my left hand — willing it to move, to twitch, to do anything — and it still lay there motionless, like it belonged to someone else.

The frustration hit like a wave.

I felt angry.

I felt broken.

I felt cheated.

I felt like screaming, but all I could do was stare at my useless limb and wonder how the hell I was going to live like this.

A nurse saw the look on my face and sat down beside me.

"Recovery isn't a straight line, Robert. You'll have bad days. But you'll have wins too. And those wins will matter more than you think."

I didn't believe her yet.

The First Small Victory

On the third day of rehab — after hours of exercises, stretches, and attempts that felt pointless — something happened.

I was lying in bed, exhausted, staring at my left foot.

"Come on," I whispered.

"Just move. Just a little."

And then…

a twitch.

Small.

Subtle.

Barely noticeable.

But real.

I stared at it like it was a miracle.

I tried again.

Another tiny twitch.

It was nothing compared to walking or standing or living a normal life — but it was something.

A sign that the connection between my brain and my body wasn't completely gone.

A sign that maybe, just maybe, there was a chance.

Hope Returns Slowly

Rehab didn't get easier — it got harder.

But that tiny twitch stayed with me.

It was the spark I needed.

The one thing that told me my body wasn't done fighting.

And even though the road ahead was long…

even though I didn't know how far I'd get…

even though fear still lived in my chest…

I held onto that spark.

Because sometimes recovery starts small —

so small you almost miss it.

But that's how healing works.

Quiet at first.

Then louder.

And I was just beginning to learn how to hear it.

CHAPTER TWELVE
The Long Fight to Move Again

Progress in rehab doesn't look like progress.
Not at first.
It looks like pain.
It looks like struggle.
It looks like failure — repeated, frustrating, exhausting failure.
It looks like trying a thousand times just to get one tiny win.
If waking up was the shock,
and learning I was paralyzed was the heartbreak,
then rehab was the battlefield.
This was where I had to decide who I was going to be now —
the man who gave up,
or the man who kept swinging even when everything hurt.

The Pain Was Constant

Every morning started with stiffness — a deep, aching heaviness in muscles that hadn't moved in weeks.
My left leg felt like it was made of stone.
My left arm felt like it had been unplugged from my body.
My back burned.
My chest hurt from being shocked back to life.
Even my skin felt sore.
Pain medicine didn't take it away — it only dulled the edges.
Rehab sharpened them right back again.
There were days I woke up and thought,
I can't do this today.
But you don't get the luxury of quitting in rehab.
You either show up… or you don't get better.
So I showed up.

The Work Was Humbling

Rehab stripped me down to nothing.
There's a special kind of humbling that comes with relearning the basics:

How to sit without falling.
How to stand without collapsing.
How to shift your weight.
How to take a step that doesn't look like a fall.
How to move muscles that feel like they belong to someone else.
My right side did the heavy lifting.
My left side lagged, resisted, froze, trembled, or stayed still.
Some days it felt like trying to move a parked car with my bare hands.
The therapist would say,
"Engage your quad. Now lift."
And I would try — with everything in me — but the leg didn't move.
That kind of failure... it hits your soul.
It makes you feel weak in a way you don't want to admit.

Setbacks Hit Hard
Some days I made progress.
Some days I slid backward.
A day where I could wiggle my toes would be followed by a day where nothing moved at all.
A day where I stood for 10 seconds would be followed by a day where I collapsed into the therapist's arms.
Setbacks mess with your head.
They make you question every step forward.
They whisper lies like:
You're never getting better.
This is permanent.
You'll never walk again.
I fought those thoughts as hard as I fought the physical pain.
But they were always there.

The Emotional Battles Were Worse
Rehab wasn't just a physical fight — it was mental warfare.
I felt embarrassed needing help for everything.
I felt angry that my body refused to cooperate.

I felt guilty that my family had to watch me struggle.
I felt frustrated that progress came so slowly.
I felt afraid that this was my new life forever.
There were days I broke down.
Days the frustration boiled over.
Days I snapped at therapists, nurses, even myself.
But every time I hit that wall, someone was there —
a nurse, a therapist, a family member —
reminding me that recovery wasn't supposed to be pretty.
It was supposed to be hard.
And I was still here.
Still fighting.

The First Major Win
It happened on a morning when I almost didn't try.
My body felt like lead.
My brain was fogged.
My emotions were shot.
The therapist helped me sit on the edge of the bed.
"Let's try something," he said.
"Shift your weight onto your left leg."
I laughed — bitter, defeated.
"That leg doesn't do anything."
"Try."
So I took a breath.
I leaned sideways.
And for the first time…
my left leg didn't collapse.
It held — weak, shaking, barely, but it held.
The therapist smiled.
"That's progress."
I didn't smile.
I cried.
Because for the first time in weeks,
I felt hope — real hope — not the forced kind people try to give you
to make you feel better.

This came from my own body.
My own fight.
My own will.

Learning to Walk Again

The walker came next.
My right leg stepped.
My left leg dragged.
Therapists guided it with straps and their hands.
Step, slide, wobble, stop.
Step, slide, wobble, stop.
It wasn't pretty.
It wasn't fast.
It wasn't graceful.
But it was movement.
It was forward.
It was life.
And with each attempt, something inside me grew stronger —
not just the muscles,
but the belief that I wasn't done yet.

The Road Was Long... But I Was Still On It

Rehab didn't give me my life back all at once.
It gave it to me in pieces:
A twitch.
A shift.
A moment of balance.
A step with help.
A step without help.
A day without collapsing.
A night without fear.
Piece by piece,
inch by inch,
I fought my way back into myself.
The road ahead was still long.
There were more setbacks waiting.

More pain.
More frustration.
    But something had changed.
    I wasn't dying anymore.
I was fighting.
    And I wasn't fighting alone.

CHAPTER THIRTEEN
The Mental Battle

Physical pain is one thing.

But the mental battle…

that's a different kind of beast.

There were days in rehab when my body hurt more than I thought it could.

But the days that scared me most were the ones where my mind went dark.

No one warns you that recovery is just as much emotional as it is physical.

No one tells you how hard it is to look at yourself and not recognize the person staring back.

No one prepares you for the grief — the grief of losing the life you used to have.

I wasn't just fighting paralysis.

I was fighting myself.

The Guilt Hit First

Guilt came in waves — heavy, relentless, suffocating.

Guilt for trusting the wrong doctors.

Guilt for taking pills I didn't know were dangerous together.

Guilt for ignoring the warning signs my body tried to give me.

Guilt for putting my parents, my daughter, and my family through hell.

Guilt for almost leaving them — not by choice, but by consequence.

Every time I saw the look in my mom's eyes — relief mixed with fear — the guilt tightened around my chest.

Every time my dad stood silently by my bed, trying to be strong, I felt guilty for making him hurt.

Every time my daughter sat beside me, whispering, "Daddy, I'm so glad you woke up," it broke me and healed me all at once.

Guilt is heavy.

Heavier than paralysis.

Heavier than pain.

Then Came the Depression

People think depression looks like sadness.
But mine looked like emptiness — like being inside a room with no windows, no air, and no way out.

I'd lie in bed wondering if my life was over.
Not physically — spiritually.

Was I still a father?
Was I still a son?
Was I still a man?
Was I ever going to walk again?
Was anyone going to look at me the same?
Would I ever look at myself the same?

Rehab demanded strength I didn't always have.
And on the days I failed — the days I couldn't move, couldn't balance, couldn't stop crying — the depression dug deeper.

Some nights I prayed.
Some nights I begged God for another chance.
Some nights I stared at the ceiling, wondering why I survived when so many people don't.

The truth hit hard:
Survival doesn't feel like a blessing when you're still broken.

The Anger Followed

Anger is easier than fear.
It's louder.
It gives you something to hold on to.

I got angry at myself.
Angry at the pills.
Angry at the doctors.
Angry at the pharmacies that didn't catch the dangerous combination.
Angry at my body for failing.
Angry at the world for moving on while I was stuck in a bed learning how to lift a spoon.

There were days I snapped at nurses.

Days I cursed under my breath.

Days I wanted to rip the monitors off and quit everything.

Anger burned, but it also pushed me.

It gave me energy when nothing else did.

Anger, in its own twisted way, kept me alive.

But it couldn't heal me.

Then Something Shifted

Healing doesn't happen all at once.

It happens in tiny moments that don't look like healing at all.

The moment my daughter held my hand and whispered,

"I'm proud of you, Dad."

The moment my mom kissed my forehead like she did when I was a boy and told me,

"You're stronger than you think."

The moment my dad wiped a tear from his eye — something he never did — and said quietly,

"You're gonna get through this, Son."

The moment a therapist said,

"You took two steps today — you didn't think you ever would."

The moment I looked at my left leg and realized it twitched without being asked.

The moment I felt my faith return — not loud, not dramatic, but steady.

Slowly, the anger softened.

The depression lightened.

The guilt loosened.

And something else began to grow in its place.

Forgiveness Was the Hardest Part

Not forgiveness for the system that failed me.

Not forgiveness for the doctors who didn't warn me.

Not forgiveness for the mess that almost killed me.

Forgiveness for myself.

Forgiving myself for not knowing better.

For being human.

For trusting people who didn't protect me.
For breaking.
For surviving.
For needing time to heal.
　　It took longer than moving my leg.
Longer than sitting up.
Longer than taking my first steps.
　　But eventually, forgiveness came —
quietly, gently, like a breath I didn't know I'd been holding.

The Mental Battle Didn't End… but I Started Winning

　　Recovery wasn't a straight line.
My emotions still swung.
My fear still crept in.
My doubts still tried to take over.
　　But I wasn't drowning anymore.
　　I was fighting.
Not just with my body — with my mind.
And for the first time since the collapse, I believed I could win.
　　Rehab was rebuilding my muscles.
But this — the mental battle —
this was rebuilding **me**.

CHAPTER FOURTEEN
The Day They Told Me I Might Walk Again

Hope is a strange thing.

It doesn't arrive all at once.

It doesn't kick down the door and announce itself.

It shows up quietly — in whispers, in moments, in unexpected places.

Up until that day, everything in rehab had felt uncertain.

Every improvement came with a warning.

Every step forward came with a "maybe" attached.

No one made promises.

No one gave guarantees.

I understood why.

They didn't know how far the damage went.

They didn't know what would come back.

They didn't know if my left side would reconnect or stay silent forever.

But on that day, something changed.

The Assessment

A doctor and two therapists walked into my room early in the morning.

I remember thinking their faces looked different — not casual, not routine, almost… hopeful.

They told me they wanted to run an assessment — something more detailed than the daily exercises, something that measured actual neurological connection.

I didn't expect much.

I had gotten used to disappointment.

I had gotten used to hearing,

"Not yet,"

"Maybe later,"

"We'll keep trying."

They positioned me on the edge of the bed, supported my back, and tested my reflexes, my grip strength, my leg control, my core stability.

Then came the big test:

"Robert, try lifting your left leg for us."

I took a breath.

Focused.

Pushed.

And…

nothing.

But then the therapist said,

"Wait… try again."

So I did.

And this time, there was movement.

Small.

Barely noticeable.

But real.

A lift — uneven, shaky, weak — but a lift.

The therapist looked at the doctor with a surprised smile.

"That's new."

The Words That Changed Everything

The doctor knelt beside me, putting a hand on my shoulder.

"Robert," he said, his voice softer than I'd ever heard it,

"I want to be careful with what I say… but this is a very good sign."

I stared at him, not sure I understood.

He continued,

"You have neurological response in your left leg. Not much yet, but enough to tell us something important."

My heart pounded.

"What?" I whispered.

He took a breath — steady, deliberate — like he wanted to get the words right.

"You may walk again."

For a moment, the world stopped.

The machines kept beeping.

The therapists kept standing there.

The fluorescent light buzzed above us.

But inside me, something broke open.

"Might" wasn't a promise.

But after weeks of "we don't know,"

after days of fearing I'd never move normally again,

after lying in a bed wondering if my life had ended without a funeral —

"might" felt like a miracle.

My Reaction Wasn't What I Expected

I didn't shout.

I didn't cheer.

I didn't smile.

I cried.

Not loud.

Not dramatic.

Just tears rolling down my face — quiet, steady, full of weeks of fear and doubt and pain.

The therapist squeezed my shoulder.

"You earned this," she said.

"This isn't luck. This is you fighting."

But I didn't feel strong.

I felt fragile — like hope was something I wasn't sure I deserved yet.

Still... it was there.

Hope was there.

Calling My Family

My mom was the first person I told.

She rushed into the room as soon as she saw the tears on my face, thinking something was wrong.

"They said... I might walk again," I managed to say.

She froze.

Her eyes filled instantly.

She reached for my hand like she had been waiting for that sentence since the moment I collapsed.

"Bobby," she whispered, "I knew it. I knew you would fight your way back."

My dad came next — eyes wet, jaw clenched, doing everything he could not to break down.

He put a hand on my shoulder and said the same words he told me as a kid:

"That's my boy."

My daughter hugged me gently, careful of the wires and tubes. She didn't say anything at first — she just held on.

Then she whispered,

"I knew you weren't done yet."

Those moments matter.

They stay with you.

They become anchors in the storm.

A Spark Reignited

That single sentence — *You might walk again* — didn't solve everything.

My leg was still weak.

My arm was still stubborn.

Rehab was still brutal.

Progress was still slow.

But now...

there was purpose.

There was possibility.

There was a reason to push harder.

For the first time since waking up, the future didn't feel like a blank wall.

It felt like a door.

And for the first time...

it felt like it might open.

CHAPTER FIFTEEN
The First Independent Steps

They tell you recovery comes in stages.
That progress is measured in inches, not miles.
That small wins add up over time.

But nothing — **nothing** — prepares you for the moment when "maybe" becomes movement.

The day I took my first independent steps wasn't neat or pretty or cinematic.
It wasn't a miracle happening in slow motion.
It was messy, shaky, emotional, and almost unbelievable.

But it was real.
And it changed everything.

It Started Like Any Other Rehab Day

I was already exhausted before therapy began.
My left leg was stiff.
My arm tingled with that strange half-numb, half-electric sensation that meant nerves were trying to reconnect.
My mind was foggy from pain and effort.

The therapist rolled in the walker, same as always, and said, "Let's warm up. Just like we've been doing."

I nodded, but inside, I felt like quitting.
I was tired of the daily grind, tired of falling, tired of lifting a leg that didn't want to lift.

I was tired of being tired.

But I pushed anyway.

Right leg forward.
Left leg guided by the therapist.
Weight shift.
Pause.
Try again.

The same steps I'd been doing for weeks.
But something felt different that morning.
Not big — subtle.

Like my leg was listening just a little more closely.

The Moment Everything Shifted

During a rest break, the therapist knelt beside me.

"Okay, Robert," she said, "I want to try something new."

New usually meant harder.

Harder usually meant pain.

But I nodded anyway.

"I want you to try taking a step without us holding your left side."

I stared at her like she was asking me to jump to the moon.

"By myself?"

She smiled. "With the walker — yes."

"No hands on your leg?"

"No hands."

My heart pounded.

Fear and hope collided hard in my chest.

She positioned the walker in front of me.

Locked it.

Made sure my balance was centered.

"Whenever you're ready," she said.

I took a breath.

I focused.

I told my brain:

Left leg, lift.

Left leg, move.

Left leg, help me.

And for the first time…

it did.

Weakly.

Shakily.

Barely.

But it moved.

It lifted off the ground.

It stepped forward.

It didn't collapse.

The therapist gasped.
The other therapist stepped back in shock.

"Robert... that was YOU. All you."

I froze — not from fear, but from disbelief.

I had moved my left leg.

I did.

Not the therapist's hand.

Not a strap.

Not luck.

Me.

Then Came the Second Step

"Try again," the therapist said, voice trembling.

I tightened my grip on the walker.

Shifted my weight.

Focused hard enough to make my head spin.

And the second step happened.

Not perfect.

Not steady.

But real.

The therapist wiped her eyes.

"Robert... you're walking."

I wasn't, not fully — not like before.

But I took a third step.

Then a fourth.

Each one shaky, uneven, slow.

But they were mine.

I wasn't being held up.

I wasn't being guided.

I wasn't being lifted.

I was walking.

I Broke Down

I didn't mean to.

I didn't want to.

But the emotion hit so hard I couldn't hold it in.

Tears came fast — full, heavy, unstoppable.

Not tears of sadness.

Not tears of fear.

Tears of **rebirth**.

The therapists let me cry.

They didn't interrupt.

They didn't push.

They just let me feel the weight of the moment.

Because they knew —

this was more than a step.

This was a life coming back.

The Call

My first call was to my mom.

She answered on the first ring.

"Bobby? You okay?"

I tried to speak, but the words came out broken, choked.

"Mom... I walked."

Silence.

Then her voice cracked so hard I felt it in my chest.

"Oh my God... oh my sweet boy... I knew you would. I knew it."

My dad came on next — voice steady, proud, fighting tears.

"That's my son. I told you you weren't done."

And my daughter —

she sobbed.

Not from worry this time — from hope.

"Daddy... I'm so proud of you."

It Was Only a Few Steps... But It Was Everything

I didn't walk a mile.

I didn't run.

I didn't dance.

I took **four steps** — slow, shaky, uneven, imperfect.

But those four steps were more powerful than anything I'd done in my entire life.

They were proof.

Proof that recovery wasn't just theoretical.

Proof that my body wasn't finished.
Proof that I had more chapters left to live.
Proof that I wasn't done fighting.

Those steps weren't just steps.

They were a promise.

A promise that the man I used to be wasn't gone —
just rebuilding, stronger than before.

CHAPTER SIXTEEN
Regaining Strength & Leaving the Hospital

Those first independent steps changed something inside me.
They didn't erase the pain, the fear, or the uncertainty — but they lit a fire.
A quiet fire, the kind that burns steady instead of wild.
For the first time, I felt like I wasn't just surviving.
I was rebuilding.
But the fight wasn't over.
In many ways, it was just beginning.

The Grind of Getting Stronger
Walking once was a victory.
Walking again was a battle.
Walking consistently was a war.
Every day the therapists pushed me farther:
Standing without the walker for a few seconds.
Balancing with one hand on the rail.
Taking steps without someone guiding my left leg.
Moving through the parallel bars.
Transferring from bed to chair without collapsing.
My muscles ached constantly.
My back throbbed.
My left arm wouldn't cooperate.
My left leg trembled like it was learning to exist all over again.
Some days I moved forward.
Some days I slid back.
Some days I couldn't stop crying.
But I never stopped showing up.
Even when it hurt.
Even when I was exhausted.
Even when I doubted myself.
Even when the fear whispered that I'd relapse into paralysis.
Every step I took was a declaration:
I'm still here.

I'm still fighting.
I'm not done.

The Therapists Became Family

Rehab therapists are different.
They see you at your lowest — broken, weak, frustrated, terrified.
They push you when you hate them.
They encourage you when you're ready to quit.
They celebrate wins with you like they're their own.
They don't just rebuild bodies —
they rebuild spirits.
One therapist told me something I never forgot:
"Your body remembers how to be strong.
We just have to remind it."
And every day, they reminded me.
Over and over.

Strength Came in Pieces

Strength didn't come back all at once.
It returned in fragments:
The day I stood up without wobbling.
The day I shifted weight onto my left leg.
The day I lifted my left arm two inches off the bed.
The day I reached a cup with my left hand.
The day I took twelve steps without the walker.
Each moment was small.
Each moment was massive.
Because every victory whispered:
"You're coming back."

The Conversation About Leaving

One afternoon, the doctor came in with a clipboard, a smile, and news I didn't expect.
"Robert," he said, "we're preparing your discharge plan."
The room went still.
"Discharge?" I asked.
"Yes. You're medically stable. You're strong enough. You're ready."

For weeks, the hospital had been my entire world — the machines, the therapists, the alarms, the hallways, the routines. Leaving meant stepping into a world I wasn't sure I belonged to anymore.

A world that had moved on without me.

A world where I wasn't the same man I used to be.

A world I'd have to learn how to navigate with new limitations.

Fear twisted in my stomach.

"What if I'm not ready?"

"You are," he said firmly.

"And you won't be alone."

Telling My Family

My mom cried.

My dad's eyes softened in a way that told me he'd been waiting for this moment since the collapse.

My daughter hugged me gently, whispering,

"I'm so glad you're coming home, Daddy."

Their faces told a story I couldn't see —

the relief, the exhaustion, the fear they'd carried while I drifted between life and death.

This wasn't just my victory.

It was theirs.

The Last Rehab Session

On the morning of discharge, my therapist asked:

"You want to take one more walk before you leave?"

I nodded.

We walked the hallway — slow, steady, my left side weak but alive.

Every staff member who passed by smiled, clapped, or gave a nod.

They had all seen me at my worst.

Now they were seeing me take steps toward the rest of my life.

Leaving the Hospital

They wheeled me to the exit even though I could walk — policy. But when the doors opened and the sunlight hit my face, something inside me cracked open again.

I had entered this hospital unconscious, dying, nearly gone.
I was leaving awake, alive, walking, grateful.

The air felt different.
The sky looked brighter.
Even the breeze felt like a second chance.

My parents stood on each side of me.
My daughter hugged my arm.
And I took a deep breath — the kind of breath that means:
I survived.
Now I rebuild.

CHAPTER SEVENTEEN
Returning Home

Leaving the hospital felt like freedom.
Returning home felt like impact.
No one prepares you for the emotional punch that hits when you walk back into the place where your life fell apart.
A place that once felt familiar suddenly feels foreign.
Comfortable spaces feel haunted.
Things you used to do without thinking now look impossible.
Home wasn't home anymore.
It was the scene of the collapse.
The reminder of everything I lost.
And the place where I had to rebuild from scratch.

The First Steps Inside

Walking through the door, supported by my family, I felt the weight of it immediately.
The house was exactly as I'd left it —
the same furniture,
the same pictures on the wall,
the same smells,
the same quiet.
But I wasn't the same man walking into it.
Every corner looked different.
Every room felt heavier.
The spot where I collapsed felt like a shadow I could still see.
I paused in the doorway longer than I meant to.
My mom gently squeezed my arm.
"You're safe now, Bobby. You're home."
But safety didn't feel simple anymore.

The Shock of Independence Being Gone

People don't realize how many small things require strength, balance, coordination, and two working sides of your body.
Opening a door.

Carrying a drink.
Getting out of bed.
Sitting without falling sideways.
Taking a shower.
Putting on socks.
Picking something off the floor.
   I couldn't do any of it alone.
   Every movement was a reminder of what I'd lost.
Every task felt like a mountain.
Every stumble felt like failure.
   The frustration hit hard.
   I wanted to be grateful.
I wanted to stay positive.
I wanted to be the man who walked out of the hospital feeling hopeful.
   But being home stripped everything raw.

The Emotional Crash
   Hospitals feel structured —
people checking on you,
therapists encouraging you,
nurses keeping you alive,
machines monitoring your body.
   Home feels quiet.
   Too quiet.
   That first night, lying in my own bed, the silence was overwhelming.
I stared at the ceiling, replaying the collapse, the coma, the doctors, the pain, the rehab, the fear.
   Gratitude mixed with sadness.
Relief mixed with guilt.
Hope mixed with depression.
   And I realized something important:
   Surviving the coma was one battle.
Rehab was another.
But being home —

this was a battle of its own.

The Left Side Reality
My left leg felt heavy, unreliable.
My left arm barely responded.
I struggled to get comfortable.
Every movement required planning.
Every step had risk.
The floor felt uneven beneath me.
Light felt too bright.
My balance felt unpredictable.
One stumble could undo months of recovery.
I hated needing help.
I hated asking for anything.
I hated feeling weak in a house where I used to be strong.
But my family showed up —
patient, gentle, steady.
They didn't hover.
They didn't overwhelm.
They didn't judge.
They just supported me, step by step.

The Fear of Being Alone
The first time everyone left the room, even for a minute, panic
hit me hard.
What if I fell?
What if my leg gave out?
What if I collapsed again?
What if I needed help and couldn't call for it?
The fear sat heavy on my chest.
Survival changes you —
it rewires the way you see the world.
Everything becomes a risk.
Everything feels fragile.
I tried not to show the fear, but my daughter saw it anyway.
"Dad," she said softly, "you're safe. We're right here."

And for the first time since coming home,
I let myself breathe.

The First Night Back
Sleep didn't come easily.
Every sound made me jump.
Every memory of the collapse returned.
Every ache in my body reminded me that life wasn't normal anymore.

But in that quiet room, with my family safe downstairs, a realization hit me:
I had been given a second chance.
A real one.
Not everyone gets that.

The recovery wasn't over.
The pain wasn't over.
The fear wasn't over.

But I was home.
Alive.
Breathing.
Fighting.

And tomorrow would be another step forward —
no matter how small.

CHAPTER EIGHTEEN
The New Reality

Recovery changes when you leave the hospital.

In rehab, you're surrounded by professionals whose entire job is to support you.

At home, the world is not built for someone learning to walk again — mentally or physically.

My house felt different.

Smaller in some places.

Bigger in others.

Full of memories… but also full of reminders of what I had survived.

This was the chapter where I had to learn how to live again — not just walk, not just move, but **live**.

Home Rehab Was Nothing Like Hospital Rehab

Hospital rehab was structured.

Home rehab was unpredictable.

At the hospital, someone was there to catch me if I fell.

At home, falling meant real danger.

Every hallway felt longer.

Every step felt higher.

Every chore felt monumental.

Simple tasks became rehab exercises:

Carrying a plate to the kitchen.

Walking from the bedroom to the living room.

Getting in and out of the shower.

Climbing a single step.

Holding something with my left hand for more than a second.

These weren't just tasks — they were battles.

Home rehab wasn't measured in medical charts.

It was measured in moments:

How long I could stand before the leg trembled.

How far I could walk before my balance shifted.

Whether I could lift a cup with my left hand without dropping it.

Progress was painfully slow.
But it was progress.

The Emotional Weight at Home Hit Hard
At the hospital, I didn't have time to think.
At home, I had nothing *but* time.
Time to think.
Time to remember.
Time to worry.
Time to feel.
Depression doesn't need a reason — it finds you in the quiet.
There were mornings I didn't want to get out of bed.
Days I sat in a chair staring at the floor, wondering why I survived.
Nights where memories of the collapse replayed like a movie I couldn't turn off.
Survival guilt hit me harder at home than it ever did in rehab.
Why me?
Why did I wake up when so many don't?
Why was I spared?
I didn't have answers.
But the questions stayed.

My Body Felt Like a Stranger
Some days my left leg responded.
Some days it didn't.
Some days it twitched like electricity was traveling through it.
Other days it felt dead again.
The inconsistency messed with my head.
I'd make progress one day and lose it the next.
And every setback felt like betrayal — like my body was teasing me with hope and then pulling it away.
There were moments I slammed my fist into the mattress out of frustration.
Moments I cursed the pills that almost killed me.
Moments I hated myself for trusting the wrong people.
Moments I felt weak — not physically, but emotionally.

But every time I struggled, I reminded myself:
"I didn't come this far to quit."

The Small Breakthroughs Were Everything

Progress at home didn't come in big victories — it came in tiny moments:

The first time I stood from the couch without holding onto something.

The first time I brushed my teeth with my left hand — shaky, messy, but possible.

The first time I walked from one end of the house to the other without stopping.

The first time I laughed again — really laughed.

The first time I felt like me.

Those moments mattered.

They were the proof that the fight wasn't in vain.

They were reminders that healing wasn't a fantasy — it was happening, quietly, slowly, but surely.

Learning to Accept the New Version of Myself

I wasn't the same man who collapsed.

I wasn't the same man who walked into the hospital unconscious.

I wasn't the same man who fought through rehab.

I was someone in between — someone rebuilding himself piece by piece.

Learning to accept that version of me took time.

I missed the old strength, the old independence, the old confidence.

I missed moving without thinking.

I missed living without fear.

But I also saw something else:

I saw a man who survived what should have killed him.

A man who took his first steps again after being told he might never move.

A man who fought through the darkest moments and refused to quit.

Accepting the "new me" wasn't weakness.
It was courage.

A Quiet Promise to Myself

One night, sitting alone, thinking about everything I'd been through —
the coma, the paralysis, the rehab, the fear, the miracles —
I made myself a promise:

I'm not going backward.
I'm not giving up.
I'm not wasting this second chance.

I didn't know what the rest of recovery would look like.
I didn't know how far I'd get.
I didn't know what setbacks were still waiting for me.

But I knew one thing with absolute certainty:

I was alive.
I was healing.
And I was not done.

CHAPTER NINETEEN
Rediscovering Purpose

There's a moment in recovery when you realize the fight isn't just about walking again, or moving your arm, or regaining strength —
it's about rediscovering **who you are** after everything you've survived.

The body heals in steps.
The mind heals in layers.
But purpose... purpose comes back slowly, quietly, like a light flickering on after a long outage.

Chapter Nineteen is where the question changed from:
"How do I survive?"
to
"What do I do with the life I got back?"

Living With the New Version of Me

By this point, I could walk short distances without collapsing.
I could stand a little steadier.
I could move my left leg with more confidence — not perfect, but present.
My left arm was still stubborn, still unpredictable, still weak, but it was improving.

But movement wasn't the same as living.
The world felt different after the coma.
Colors seemed sharper.
Time felt more valuable.
People looked more important.
Pain didn't define me the way it once did.
And survival wasn't enough — I wanted meaning.

But rediscovering purpose is hard when you barely recognize yourself.
Some days I felt strong.
Some days I felt useless.
Some days I felt like a miracle.

Some days I felt like a burden.

The mental battle continued long after the hospital doors closed behind me.

The First Signs That I Still Had a Future

Purpose didn't return in a flash.

It came in small moments — quiet reminders that my life was still mine.

A client called just to say they were praying for me.

A friend stopped by and told me he needed my advice.

My daughter asked me to help her with something, treating me like the dad I had always been.

My family started asking me questions about insurance like they always had — like nothing had changed.

Every time someone believed I still mattered,

a piece of me came back.

The collapse had taken my body.

But it hadn't taken my mind.

And it sure as hell didn't take my heart.

The Feeling of Responsibility Returning

Before the coma, stress had been a weight.

After the coma, responsibility became something different — not a burden, but a calling.

I wasn't the same man I had been before all this.

I was slower.

More careful.

More thoughtful.

More aware.

And with that awareness came a realization:

I survived for a reason.

I didn't get that second chance by accident.

A rookie paramedic refused to give up on me.

Doctors fought for me.

My family prayed for me.

God kept me alive when I had no strength left.

I couldn't treat that like nothing.
I had to do something with it.

The Moment Things Started Coming Back Together
One morning, while sitting at the table with my notebook, I felt something I hadn't felt in months:
Purpose.
It hit me in a simple thought:
"I want to help people again."
Not just with insurance.
Not just with policies.
Not just with business.
I wanted to help people avoid what I went through.
I wanted to tell my story.
I wanted to warn others about the dangers of pill mills, bad prescriptions, and medical negligence.
I wanted to show people, especially men who hide their pain, that asking for help is strength — not weakness.
For the first time since waking up,
I felt like I had a mission again.

Slowly Rebuilding My Life
Healing wasn't fast.
It wasn't clean.
It wasn't dramatic.
But I rebuilt my life piece by piece:
Walking farther every day.
Practicing balance.
Using my left hand for small tasks.
Taking control of my medications.
Reconnecting with friends.
Getting back into my business.
Finding joy in everyday life.
Feeling my faith grow stronger.
Every day I woke up, I was reminded:
I wasn't supposed to be here.

But I was.
And I had work to do.

Purpose Makes You Stronger Than Any Rehab
Rehab rebuilt my muscles.
Family rebuilt my hope.
But purpose —
purpose rebuilt my soul.
I wasn't living in survival mode anymore.
I wasn't drowning in fear anymore.
I wasn't haunted by the collapse the same way.
I had something to chase.
Something to build.
Something to contribute.
For the first time since I opened my eyes in the hospital,
I wasn't just healing…
I was becoming myself again.
And that made everything I'd gone through —
the pain, the fear, the darkness, the paralysis, the fight —
mean something.

CHAPTER TWENTY
Full Circle

There comes a moment after trauma when you look at your life —
everything you lost, everything you gained, everything you survived —
and you realize you're not the same person who collapsed on that floor.

You're stronger.
You're wiser.
You're harder in some places, softer in others.
You're more present.
More grateful.
More aware of how fragile and how resilient life can be in the same breath.

This final chapter isn't about paralysis or recovery or even survival.

It's about the man I became because of it.

Survival Changes You

Most people think waking up from a coma is the victory.
It's not.

The real victory is what comes after —
the rebuilding, the relearning, the emotional fight, the courage to face life with a new body and a new mind.

I survived something that should have ended my life.
My family stood over me expecting the worst.
Doctors almost called my time of death.
A rookie paramedic brought me back.

You don't walk away from that unchanged.

I didn't just wake up —
I woke up a different man.

A man who understood his own vulnerability.
A man who found strength in places he didn't know existed.
A man who finally learned how precious a single day is.

And a man determined to never waste another one.

Gratitude Became My Anchor
There were days I didn't feel grateful.
Days the pain overshadowed everything.
Days I asked, "Why me?"
Days I struggled with who I was becoming.
But gratitude always found its way back —
in the moments that mattered most:
The way my mom talked to me during the coma as if I could hear every word.
The way my dad held my hand and whispered, "Come on, Son..."
The way my daughter's "Daddy?" brought me all the way back to life.
The way my sister Carrie kept everything running so my parents never had to leave my bedside.
The way Tammy flew down just to sit with me — her last act of love before she left this world.
The way my friends showed up.
The way nurses fought for me.
The way therapists believed in me long before I believed in myself.
Gratitude didn't erase the pain —
it softened it.
It gave it purpose.
It turned suffering into strength.

Reflection: What the Collapse Taught Me
The collapse taught me more about life than any peaceful moment ever could:

- That the body can fail, but the will can rise.
- That the mind can break, but the heart can rebuild.
- That family is everything — the glue when you fall apart.
- That miracles don't always look magical — sometimes they look like a rookie paramedic refusing to give up.
- That faith matters, especially in the darkest places.

-        That guilt and anger are normal, but they don't get to stay.
-        That healing isn't quick or clean — it's messy, painful, unpredictable.
-        And that a second chance isn't just given… it must be earned.

What I faced wasn't punishment.
It was awakening.

Becoming the Man I Was Meant to Be
Before the coma, I thought strength was pushing through pain at all costs.
I thought success meant working nonstop, carrying everything alone, never showing weakness.
But real strength is different.
Strength is asking for help.
Strength is letting people love you.
Strength is breaking down and standing back up.
Strength is rebuilding yourself from nothing.
Strength is surviving what should have killed you —
and choosing to *live* afterward.
I didn't just recover physically.
I recovered emotionally.
Spiritually.
Purposefully.
I became a man who knows his worth.
A man who values time more than money.
A man who loves deeper.
A man who listens more.
A man who forgives himself.
A man who wakes up every day knowing he got a second chance.
And I try to honor that chance —
in how I treat people,
in how I work,
in how I love,
in how I live.

Full Circle

I went from near death...
to a hospital bed...
to paralysis...
to rehab...
to walking again...
to rebuilding my life...
to becoming a man I'm proud to be.

Full circle isn't going back to who I was.

Full circle is becoming the person I was always meant to be —
the one who survived,
the one who fought,
the one who refused to quit.

This is my story.
My truth.
My second chance.

And if someone reading this is struggling with their own darkness —
their own collapse,
their own paralysis,
their own fight —
I hope they see this and understand:

You can come back from anything.
Even from the edge of almost gone

EPILOGUE
The Life I Choose Now

When I look back at the story you just read, it sometimes feels like it happened to another man — someone I used to be, someone who didn't know how close he was to the edge.

But that man was me.

And the only reason I'm here to tell this story is because of second chances and people who refused to let me go.

Survival has a way of stripping life down to its essentials. It removes the noise, the excuses, and the things that never really mattered. What's left is clarity.

I live differently now.

I listen to my body instead of fighting it.

I speak up instead of pushing through pain in silence.

I move slower, but with purpose.

I don't pretend I'm invincible anymore. I don't carry everything alone.

This book isn't about pills, pharmacies, or failures.

It's about survival.

It's about grace.

It's about the people who stand beside us when we can't stand on our own.

I'm not the man who almost died.

I'm the man who lived.

And every day forward is a choice — a choice to honor the life I was given back.

AUTHOR'S NOTE

I never planned to write this book.

For a long time, I wasn't sure I wanted to revisit the memories, the fear, or the guilt. Some chapters of life feel easier to leave closed.

But survival has a way of changing your perspective.

I wrote *Almost Gone* because silence helps no one. Because people are hurting quietly. Because too many stories like mine never get told.

This is my truth as I remember it — shaped by trauma, recovery, and the long road back. Some names have been changed, and some details softened, but the heart of the story remains honest.

If this book helps even one person feel less alone, then telling it was worth it.

ABOUT THE AUTHOR

Robert B. Routt is a U.S. Navy Seabee veteran, insurance professional, father, and survivor of a near-fatal medical collapse that left him in a coma and fighting to relearn how to live.

Based in Clearwater, Florida, Robert has spent more than three decades helping individuals and families navigate health, life, dental, and Medicare insurance. After surviving cardiac arrest, a coma, and partial paralysis, he felt called to share his story so others facing pain, trauma, addiction, or life-altering medical events would know they are not alone.

Almost Gone is his debut memoir and the beginning of a mission to encourage accountability, awareness, and hope — especially for those who feel one step away from losing everything.

When he's not writing or working, Robert enjoys time with his family, his girlfriend Erin, and his loyal dog, Princess.

Learn more at **www.RobertRoutt.com**

STAY CONNECTED

If this book meant something to you, I'd be honored to stay connected.

I keep things simple — no spam, no constant emails — just honest updates, future projects, and occasional reflections.

You can expect:
·   Updates on upcoming books

- Behind-the-scenes stories
- Special announcements and signed copies

Visit **www.RobertRoutt.com** to stay in touch.

Thank you for reading my story.

Thank you for carrying it forward.

— **Robert B. Routt**